Reflections of a Pensive Heart

Deepti Gupta

Presentation by *BookLeaf Publishing*

Web: www.bookleafpub.com

E-mail: info@bookleafpub.com

ISBN: 9789363315556

First edition 2024

DEDICATION

To my Father, Shri Krishan Gupta and my Mother, Sudesh Gupta.

Maa, Papa, without you, neither I nor my poems would have existed, ever. Thank you for bringing me into this world and sowing the seeds of writing in my heart.

Love you, Forever and Ever, Wherever You are!!!

ACKNOWLEDGEMENT

It is said that life is one's biggest and truest teacher, and it teaches you all the lessons through everyone you come across during your lifetime. People, who you come across have a purpose to motivate you and steer you & your thoughts in a certain direction, even if they themselves may not have awareness of the same.

So, to all individuals who ever brought a purpose, direction, motivation, or inspiration to me, I want to say thank you for being part of my life and inspiring me to pen down my thoughts.

I also want to convey my deepest gratitude to BookLeaf Publishing for being the inspiration and a partner in crime and for bringing "Reflections of a Pensive Heart" into your hands.

Most of all, I want to thank my life partner and husband, Ankur, for giving me his unconditional Love and Support to bring forth my poems to all of you. A big hug and love to my daughter and son for being my champions and my brothers for being my best critiques.

PREFACE

As you sit down at the end of a day or in a quiet moment, away from the chaos of everyday events and routines, your heart takes a leap of its own.

Have you ever found yourself turning and tossing every event of that day (and the one that just passed along), in all directions, to decide how you perceive those moments and what you feel? Really feel deep inside?

During many such quiet moments, my heart jumped out into uncertain terrains on a journey, uncharted and unknown. And in those precious moments alone, everything else kind of stopped.

It is in moments like these that the deepest thoughts and learnings of your heart and mind bubble up to the surface in absolute clarity, bringing forth life's greatest lessons and teachings.

In the next pages of this book, you will find a portion of such a treasure from my own life. My own life's greatest revelations and reflections on seemingly simple yet very complex events.

And I hope, my little treasure finds its echo, within the realms of your own hearts and your own souls. May you find yourself, resonating with the thoughts contained in the next few pages.

In Gratitude
Deepti

Shadows of the Night

In the shadows of the night
Lies the light of a pensive heart
Tossing, turning every thought
Which is this very moment's part

But what if there's not a thought
Only one big, empty void
Silence follows, your own self
Making you feel paranoid

What is it you want to see,
What is it that you, want to hear
Whom do you want to, come around
And take you in arms, holding you near

Often, you know, answers to them
Yet it's just an empty dream
'Cause lost moments are old memories
On the sheet of Life's own scheme

Thus you close your searching eyes,
Closing down every ray of light
To go back to the realm of dreams
In the Shadows of the Night!!!

Shout of a Data Team

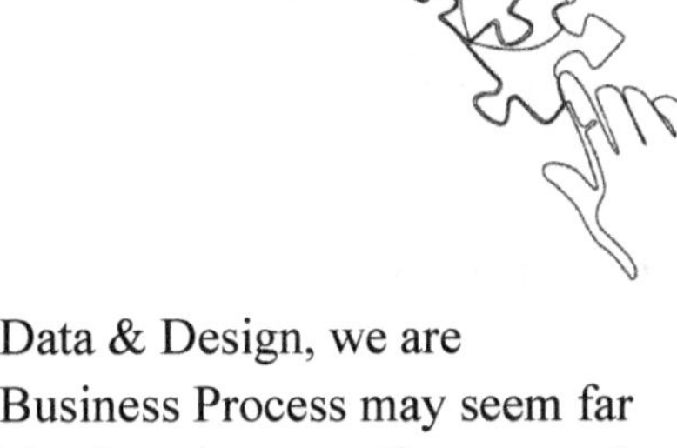

Data & Design, we are
Business Process may seem far
Yet these two are all connected
And we bring them both at par

Finance, Commerce, Sales, and Buys
We are your Data Guys
What is Target, what is Source
We know data's travel course

We know what gets pulled inside
And the data that goes out
We know every small exchange
That comes forth from data's Sprout

So, if you want to know it more
Feel free to give us a shout!!!

Heart of Success

Blue Heaven and Shining Stars
They define who we are
Different sizes, different shades
That's how we have been made

Coming together, from so far
On the tree of a common dream
Started on the path to success
Holding hands as one big team

Fought the war of utter chaos
Bringing structure to the fore
We designed the building blocks
Of this Life's very own core

Like the pieces of a puzzle
We color every broken part
To complete a pretty picture
That is Success' very own Heart!

Teachers of School

Teachers are, life's own guide
Do not judge them by their looks
They teach you lessons of life
Way beyond what's in the books

Few are soft, others are strict
But they All Love you all
Trying to prepare you
To face boldly, every fall

Guided by the teachers of class,
Tiny tots, grow up in School
Turning into Strongest Trees
Spun from Values' beautiful spool

They teach you how to laugh,
They teach you when to play
Molding you into beautiful crafts
From your own, Raw Wet Clay

They are the ones of very best
People that you come across
Bringing your treasures out
From behind your bolted doors

Know you need to cherish them
Every scolding, Every Praise
'Cause these are your precious jewels
On memories' beautiful days!

Truth and Lies

What is truth, what's a lie
What is low, what is high
They are just points of view
Taken in with a heartfelt sigh

What is Love, what is Hate
What is Karma, what is Fate
Both of them are at your service
Getting ready to make you great

Which one of the two opposites
You are going to select
That will take you on the road
To a fate that you elect

Choose wisely, dear friend
Though it's not the final end
Yet every little choice of yours
Will decide your every bend

Whether you get shining stars,
Or the stones in shades of Gray
Will depend on your choices
That you make, on the way!!!

Morning Blues

Eyes flutter and open up
Rising me from laps of sleep
As my mind keeps going back
Into the streets of longings, deep

Pictures of moments, form ahead
In the deepest depth of heart
Some are just a wishful thinking
Others have been life's own part

Passing through these narrow lanes
Nestled in my heart and soul
Heart tries to check the fabric
Of every moment, sane and foul

What they want to teach me
Which direction, Where to go
I may get the light of dawn
Or keep on thinking with a frown

In these quiet & lonely lanes
I get purpose, as I muse
Thus enabling me to rise
From the clutch of Morning Blues!

True Desire

Under the shiny roof of stars
On the calm, sheet of waves
Goes ahead the little boat
Taking light of shining rays

Not a sound all around
Only song of Boat and Row
Pushed ahead, with every thrust
Caused by dancing, water's blow

This nightly song of stars
Brings forth the deepest thought
What's that I really seek
Which my every fight has Sought

As the mind wanders through
Utter chaos of every string
Sweet nectar of moments lost
Brings forth the scent of Spring

Like the golden drops on grass
Shines the love on the Flute of heart
Dusted, rusted, or forgotten
But never have gone apart

Like a pearl in Tiny Shells
This love looks and talks to me
This is what you seek again
As you wage, the war of Thee

This is the only driving need
In every act and task of Yours
This is your true desire
In everything you have been through

With this knowledge, I close the eyes
Feeling a touch of the coldest breeze
Waking up from deepest dream
With the shout of the loudest sneeze!!!

Curtain on the Wall

Curtain, curtain on the wall
What's hidden in your fall
Springy season, Smell of Earth
What new Feelings you give birth

Shiny, Greeny leaves around
Or a Party In the Ground
What is that you wanna show
Is that meadow with the snow

Numerous feelings you invoke
In the strings of a tiny heart
Since I brought you into the home
You have become a little part

Of my life and every day
Like a tulip in the hay
You bring to us calm and peace
Like the dew of deepest pray!!!

Length of Life

Sitting in my bedroom corner
With a cushion on my knee
I try to look around
When my sight, reach to thee

With your focus on the news
You are in a different world
As your mind flies around
In the skies, like a bird

Trying to catch your sight
I just keep making wishes
As my heart plans many tricks
Just like cooking tasty dishes

And then you cast aside
Your little piece of news
And I try to guess again
What is it you, keep to muse

When I give up on the fate
Getting up to make you dine
You say something very basic
And I know you are mine

Spark in your lovely eyes
Brings to me a genuine smile
Giving me all the strength
To cover life's next tough mile

Your silent Love and Care
Is my source of all the strength
With you, I am ready to cover
Life's and World's every length!

Birth and Death

Birth and Death, on Horizon
Two shores of a Single River
Art forms of Every life
On the sheet of Time's Mirror

One reciprocates other
Like a mirror image of thee
One binds you with the life
Other tries to make you free

Birth brings you every struggle
Daily quest to keep ahead
Pushing yourself beyond the limits
And to earn your very own bread

Death is like the freedom earned
From the clutch of every pain
Churning your life's events
And the lessons yet to gain

Two halves of a single ball
They take turns to roll again
Birth leads to Death in End
And Death Brings down birth again!!!!

Nature's Craft

In the river, of the Sky
Numerous clouds keep to fly
They paint a pretty picture
Of the stones passing by

Through the surface of the water
In the river, just beneath
I can see the world of dreams
Floating down at just the sheath

Slowly, the river floats away
Making path for one big Sea
Many ships are swinging by
Making my heart feel the glee

Far away at the end of Sea
I can see a tree so Strong
Scolding off the little ones
Making bonds of Love with Young

In this calm and restful world
I find peace in my own heart
As I marvel at the wonders
Of Mother Nature's lovely craft!

Circle of Life

Seeds are sown in the womb
With the love of one's mother
In the hopes of getting one
Son, daughter, or lovely brother

As three pairs of the eyes
Keenly look at your growth
They await your arrival
With the beat of every core

Your arrival on the earth
With the party on your birth
Mark your entrance to a new world
Cheering, laughing with the mirth

River of life takes you on
Towards a path of many stones
Shaking you with every laughter
Or crushing you to the bones

And soon you find yourself
At the edge of life and death
Giving birth to your own
And losing parents, with a breath

Void of life left behind
Never gets to filled again
As you tread the path ahead
And take along the thread of pain

Yet the love of your own
Brings a shore to your heart
As you once again realize
Being only just one part

In the circle of this life
Moving along the circumference
Changing shades of roles and tasks
Along the point of time's reference

This is learning from this life
Flowing is the only way
Along the river of the life
To be molded like the clay!!!

Mirror Mirror, On the Wall

Mirror Mirror, On the Wall
As you stand up, Strong and Tall
You show us the real thing
Through the Summers, Winter, and Fall

Walking through the lanes of life
Donning roles of Mother and Wife
One gets tested all the time
On the edge of acceptance's Knife

Some would agree, with our ways
Others will keep us at the bays
Bringing clouds of darkest doubts
Cutting down on happy rays

When I come and reach You
You show me the truth as True
Shining Eyes and Subtle Smiles
Takes away all my blues

So listen, dear, beloved mirror
You bring glue to every sliver
Of my heart and of my soul
Making me free as the Fiercest river

Be with me at every step
That I'm yet to take ahead
With you as my truest friend
I can finally go to bed!!!

Mystery Lady

As I comb my hair down
On the eyes, a little frown
Alerts me down to changing air
With a feeling of traveling down

As I travel through the clouds
With my lips caught, in a bite
I arrive at beautiful lands
In a strange and unknown site

I try to find my way
Walking by the shore of bay
When I come across a beauty
Standing tall in shades of clay

Vines of grapes adore its walls
Bringing brightest hues of smiles
Purple Flowers, Scarlet Cherries
Tickle my heart's every aisle

Standing at the castle's door
Lady with the Whitest hair
Calls my name and asks to come
In the house and, to the fair

As I walk and reach to beach
At the backside of the house
Something catches sight of eyes
And I get to see my spouse

Standing tall, his handsome Self
With his hair Gray and White
He directs me once again
To the lady, on my right

She looks very known to me
With a light in lovely eyes
I recognize future self
As I take some deepest sighs

She holds my hands again
Takes me up to my own room
Draped in shades of Pink & Blues
And the flowers, in the bloom

As she raises her, hand to me
Touching gently my heart
I hear the sweetest whisper
Making alive my every part

And I know that this is mine
Yet to come in times ahead
Life full of Love and Laughter
As I open, eyes in bed!!!

The Rainbow

In Victory and Defeat
In the Rains and the heat
Life simply keeps to go
As your heart, keeps to beat

You may feel a happy mood
Or a smile may look so mute
Take a step, still ahead
As you gather, your own chute

Gather every string together
Make again a beautiful net
As you work through every knot
Life will move on, I can bet

New doors and new horizons
You will find, once again
New journey on a new path
Will take away all your pain

And the rains of your labor
On the path of highs and lows
Will give way to Sun to Shine
With the beauty of Rain's own bows!!!

Dear Cartoon!

Cartoon, Cartoon on the Screen
Where were you, how you've been
I keep waiting, just for you
With the eyes and breath so keen

Every day and every night
I search for those little breaks
When I can switch on the screen
Taking me to the world of Snakes

Or to the world of Dinosaurs
Small, Medium, and so huge
They ignite my little mind
And I finally get Refuge

From the studies and the chores
And from Mother's little tasks
While I feel like a real Hero
Wearing the strongest, finest masks

That's why I love you so
Running to you at every time
Spending my time with you
Looks like worth every dime!!!

Mouse in House

Dear room, in the house
Have you seen my little mouse
With the shiny, smallest tail
Wearing one Gray, Reddish blouse

It's my favorite little toy
That my father gave to me
With the love of his own heart
And the warmest, Widest glee

I had kept it on the desk
Right beside, Big Fat book
I have searched for it everywhere
In all the corners, every nook

Heart of mine is sounding beats
And the tiny eyes have tears
As the feeling of the loss
Raises clouds of all the fears

Oh my dear, there you are
Hidden among the shiny stars
At the bottom of the box
Overflowing with my cars

Thank you room, for taking care
Of my shiny little mouse
Let me go and help mother
In cleaning the rest of the house!!!

Skeletons in Hidden Cupboard

Skeletons, in my cupboard
Hidden away on the topmost shelf
Makes me scared very often
Casting doubts on my own self

Past mistakes of the forgotten past
Missed out goals of tender heart
Every dirty push and pull
Which has been my life's own part

Come to mind when sitting alone
From the days, battered and gone
They crush heart with every force
Of the guilt, sharp as a stone

Wish I could have changed old days
And covered across the bays
Thousand miles of hurt and pain
And to soak in Happy Rays

Of the Deepest love and hugs
Cheering us with Coffee's mugs
Maybe we could have spent more time
On memories' softest rugs

Now that you have gone away
All my secrets lay covered
Hidden away on the topmost shelf
Of my bleak and blue cupboard!!!

Dear Mother

Dear Mother, in the heavens
Do you ever call my name
Do you still remember me
And do love me, just the same

Do you still know when I'm hurt
Shedding tears from pools of eyes
Do you still know, in your heart
When I have taken my deepest sighs

Do your ears still hear the sound
Of the voices, of my heart
Do you still feel the touch of me
As I finally let you part

'Cause for me, you still are here
Whispering, Guiding all the way
I still feel you, in my core
That has come from your own clay

You are here, yet you're not
On my life's broken boat
As I say to you, byes again
With a heavy heart and throat

You be happy, where you are
Keep going with lovely smiles
Once again, I'll come to you
Covering Life's thousand miles

Once again, we will be one
In the garden, under the sun
Once again to play together
And have moments of the fun!!!

Dew on Pines

In my little, lonely world
Hearing the sound of unsaid words
Heart of mine got always full
With tears of wounded birds

Of my deepest, hidden wishes,
Dreams, Desires, and the hopes
While my life was always bound
With the Safety-net's tight ropes

Work and Home were two horizons
On the longest river of the day
False bravado was my weapon
Keeping the fears at the bay

And then life chose to bring
Most shattering wave to me
Shaking roots of my own guard
And the prison, built on Sea

Piece-by-Piece and Nail-by-Nail
Chirped away my every fear
As through the first rays of the Sun
I felt the warmth of Love's own Tear

Like the Castles, on the Hills
And the Meadows, in the stills
With your love, I painted Life
Since the day I became your wife

You opened the door for me
Towards Family and Friends
Holding me with your strength
Through the churns and deadly bends

Now I have you and the kids
Testing me and patience of mine
Yet I love your little teasing
And Your Smiles' brightest Shine

May we always stay together
In this life and those ahead
With you, I can face the world
And every fear in my head

You are my heart and soul
You are like my rhythm divine
In your arms, I rest in peace
Like the dew on Leaves of Pine!!

Drops of Rain

Room full of Smiles and Laughs
On this family's Memory Graph
Everyone around the table
Sitting together in a circle half

Raises the bar of happiness
In our lives and in our hearts
Childish fights and playful teases
Add to the Jewels on, memory's cart

World seems to come together
Getting frozen in this time
Every second, spent like this
Radiates fragrance, just like Thyme

When I come back, to my home
Take a nap on soft pillows
I dream of a flowing river
In the forest of Willows

Strings of Love and care abound
Touch the deepest spots of the heart
Filling my soul with the knowledge
That we all are different parts

Of one single source of light
Bright like the stars of night
We will always stay together
In the hills and gardens bright

With this thought, I rest again
Free of every fear and pain
Listening to the sound so sweet
Of the drumming, drops of rain!!

Congratulations

One Dream, One Desire
Every stroke of Burning Fire
In the hearts of Us and Thee
Sowed the seeds of Success's tree

Soil, Water, Sun, and Wind
Every Bruise & Knee that's skinned
Marked the little growing plant
With Success's own, little chant

Today marks the first harvest
Reaping fruits of dedication
Making everyone so proud
Full of Joy and Strong Elation

Good wishes are pouring in
Full of Pride and Strong Emotions
This poem is our own way
To wish you all Congratulations!

Memory of the Mind

From the deepest depths of heart
Come out the coldest sighs
As the soul navigates
Through life's Lows and the Highs

Forgotten are ways of the past
Cross-Roads with Trees around
When the loudest cheers were
War horns of games, on ground

Pebbles, Seeds, and Flower buds
Were the toys in tiny hands
Everyone would come together
For the Fruits from Forest Bands

Gone are those, days and nights
Of such laughter and lots of fun
As we tried to stay upright
On this life's course of run

Gone are now our parents
Lost in time are all old friends
Today's days are full of measures
Of our Success's latest trends

Heart and Soul still yearn for
Lost pearls of days and nights
When small were the dreams and hopes
Everything was just so right

Time is a healer of the wounds
Someone told us in the past
Time would take away your pain
Making it right, at the last

But I think I know the truth
Life is a circle of the Pain
That comes with every success
As the price of every gain

Like the waves of Sound and Sea
Pain and Gain are just two peaks
Of a single thread of Truth
Floating through Life's own Creeks

Accept the Truth and move ahead
Carrying every thought along
Fill with Knowledge, your Voids
To know the right from the wrong

In the end, you would be gone
Leaving everything behind
Turning yourself in a wave
Called as Memory of the Mind!